T0064396

INDIAN PARENTS HAVE
INDIAN LOOKING CHILDREN

20 Simple yet Powerful Management Lessons

Zach Cherian

PARTRIDGE
A Penguin Random House Company

To order additional copies of this book, contact
Partridge India
000 800 10062 62
www.partridgepublishing.com/india
orders.india@partridgepublishing.com

TABLE OF CONTENTS

IT HAPPENED BECAUSE YOU CARED. THANK YOU

I'd like to dedicate this book to three sets of very special people.

First, I want to dedicate this to the many managers I have worked for and the mentors I have worked with over the years. I have learnt a lot from you, and I hope you see yourself in the pages of this book. Thank You Ch Srinivas, Teresa Roche, Christopher Goh, Parmeet Ahuja, Rohana Weiler, Angela Cheong, Jayantika Dave, Pritash Mathur, Indira Screymour, Sanjeev Sethi, Kapil Chopra, Rajesh Ganotra and Arun Kumar. You took the time to teach me, and there's nothing I can ever do to repay you.

Second, to the many wonderful friends I have worked with over the years and have had the pleasure of calling 'my team'. Thank you very much. On many occasions working with me must have been so tough. I am sorry. Thank you for giving your best in every situation, and always striving to be better-than-before.

Finally, and most importantly, I'd like to thank my family of three of the most beautiful women in this world—my wife Ujwala, my daughter Zara and my daughter Zada. I love you. You give me reason to give my best, and to hope in times of confusion and anxiety. I owe you everything and I love you so much.

FOREWORD

"Learn everything you can, anytime you
can, from anyone you can—there will
always come a time when you will be
grateful you did."

Sarah Caldwell

This is a book about a leadership journey and it is a remarkable one at that. I have known Zach Cherian for several years and he is a highly respected, admired and loved leader by so many of us. What is compelling is Zach's ability to reflect deeply on what he has learned from all of his experiences to date and to cull key insights that are meaningful and accessible.

As I thought about what to say in the foreword, I contemplated on something Zach says in his introduction about how many books there are about leadership and like Zach, I read many every year. I was once told by a professor at a major university that there was nothing more to learn about leadership and that everything anyone needed to know had been said already. I remember leaving the conversation thinking that this did not seem possible. I do believe there are some fundamental principles about leading others that stand the test of time and yet in a world of unending change, I simply could not imagine there would not be more stories that would shed light on the path of a leader. And this book is definitely one that can captivate readers by inviting them over to dinner, where a meal of stories are shared and lessons learned that are most satisfying.

Zach opens his head and his heart to the numerous situations he has been in and it takes a rare individual to live the quote by Sarah Caldwell and yet Zach does. To do so, one must be open and curious; one must be willing to sort through all that is happening to find what is important and worth carrying on the trip forward. I can only imagine if Zach had written all he has learned one might need a rolling suitcase of a large size; however given his intention was for this book to serve as a companion along the way almost like a guide book that helps you know what is important to see, he focuses on twenty insights. And he lets you understand the context in which he found each of these treasures.

I found myself pausing after each insight and thinking if I had learned that particular lesson yet, and if so, had I applied it well? I thought about what was my favorite lesson and kept flipping back and forth and decided each one was important to remember.

This book not only gave me some new insights about leadership, it made me think about the power of reflection and taking time to write what I am learning so that each lesson really "sticks" and becomes a choice about how one chooses to lead.

Zach has been developing himself and others for a long time and similar to his beliefs, I do believe one can learn to lead and it begins within. Leading others starts with leading one's self, which is what Zach has done and continues to do. Zach chose to be present to what came his way and he also chose to be conscious. This way of being that comes naturally to Zach is perhaps the prerequisite that all of us must have—the willingness to stay awake, continuously learn and to make each experience one that can help us along the way.

Zach shows us how to do this with this book. Readers will not only get some great leadership lessons that are worth knowing, but they will also see how one can learn how to lead. Zach shows us the way and we are all the better for it. He writes in a way that makes me want to follow and walk behind him at times and alongside him always.

On my book shelves and in my mobile devices are some of my favorite books about leadership and this one has a prominent place where I can "pick it up" easily.

I will welcome the next book by Zach as I am quite certain that the way he leads his life will bring more stories, more insights and more goodness to the rest of us.

Dr. Teresa Roche
Vice President and Chief Learning Officer,
Agilent Technologies
December 2013

INTRODUCTION

I took nine and a half years to write this book. At this point I don't know how many pages this book is going to have, but it'll probably be about ninety. Ninety pages in nine and a half years don't sound 'enough', I know. However, this is not a collection of all that I've learnt and done in my career of about sixteen years, it's simply about key insights.

Insights don't come every day. In fact, as I realized while writing this book, sometimes you get an insight only once in six months, or a year. But you know that when you really get an insight, it hits you hard, it stays with you, and it can change the way you see things, and act in different situations.

It's those twenty hard-hitting experiences and insights that stayed with me that I've captured in this book, and am fortunate to share with you.

I read somewhere that each year about 2000 'management' books get published. That's a lot of books. I read a lot of management books too; not 2000 every year, but quite a few anyway, and I've found all of those have great learning and insight. I don't want to even attempt to pitch this book as anyway 'better' than them. I do hope, though, that you think this book is slightly 'different'.

Being a manager is tough. Sometimes, it's very tough. You have to really want to be a manager to play this sport, else it can consume you. But even when you want to do a good job, sometimes circumstances get the better of you, and you feel stuck. The pressure of expectations from all quarters can be very overwhelming. I hope you will find some peace reading this book by knowing that you're not alone.

I believe leaders can be made. I've trained thousands of managers in my career, and some of them didn't look like they were 'made' for this. Yet, with humility in their hearts, they learnt something, got better, and learnt some more, and got even better. Now I see some of them leading large teams in large organizations, and doing a great job at that.

I hope you'll see this book at least as a temporary companion in your journey to greatness as a manager. I don't mean to say that I'm a great manager just because I wrote this book. I mean that we're all learners, and the learning never ends.

Best of luck. I hope you create teams that are driven by good values, and create value for the organizations you work for. Enjoy!

INDIAN PARENTS HAVE INDIAN LOOKING CHILDREN

> You will know them by their fruit. Do people get bunches of grapes from thorny weeds, or do they get figs from thistles? In the same way, every good tree produces good fruit, and every rotten tree produces bad fruit. A good tree can't produce bad fruit. And a rotten tree can't produce good fruit.
>
> Matthew 7: 16-18, Common English Bible

The leader drives the culture of the team. This is one of those 'period' kind of statements, so let me say it again—The LEADER drives the culture of the team.

It's a simple theory called 'reproduction'. Surprised? One time we had a pastor visit our Church to preach at the New Year Eve service. He said 'Do Indian parents have American-looking babies?' He was talking about the fact that the spiritual maturity of our children will depend on how spiritually mature we (parents) are. The concept is so true for leadership in the workplace too. Your team will be laid back, if you are laid back. Your team will be a non-performing team, if you act in an unaccountable manner.

I've worked with some pretty amazing bosses. But even pretty amazing bosses sometimes display some pretty painful behavior, and soon that becomes the OK behavior of the team. Slowly, it becomes the culture.

I remember this manager who once worked for the same company I worked for. He had a pretty bad attitude towards internal customers, even though all the work his department had to do was for internal customers. His attitude can be summarized as one thinking 'I know how to run my department. I don't want anyone to give me any feedback. Our customers are irrational and over-demanding. The best way to deal with them is to fight them or to ignore them.'

This attitude had lots of negative effects in how different people (internal customers) worked with this leader and his department. But more than anything, this leader's behavior and attitude started influencing his team's behavior and attitude. I'm not saying they changed completely, but they sometimes became arrogant when it was not warranted, just like their manager. I guess they felt it was ok, because they saw their manager behave arrogantly all the time. Eventually, the internal customers became vindictive towards this leader and his team, and would pose challenges to the team in a more 'violent' manner than they needed to. I guess that's why they say—what goes around comes around.

In such an environment, those employees of this manager who genuinely wanted to do their best for their customers felt restricted. They had to constantly make the tough choice of pleasing their customer versus pleasing their boss.

Who are your employees looking to please—your customers or you?

After a while this rather negative leader left the company, and a different manager took over the team. This new guy was a breath of fresh air. He was open, communicative, a good listener, and much more collaborative. What happened? Long story short—his team is like him now. Same people, different leader, different culture. The perceived 'value' of this department has gone up significantly because it's people changed how they think and view their customers, and that changed because the leader changed.

As a leader, you're always being watched, heard and followed. It's important to walk the talk, and to talk the talk.

I've worked for a leader who has been extremely critical and impatient with his people. Well, his whole team became a bit like him. Its obvious right—if they have to constantly save themselves from this manager, then they'll go around attacking others. But can you imagine the impact of this on the organization? Earlier, on certain sensitive topics, it was tough to work with one leader. Now it's tough to work with five. This kind of stuff is never good for the organization.

As a leader you have to think about what you say and do. Ask your customers what they see your team say and do. Bottom line—get a sense check somehow, and be willing to make at least some changes that will help you, your team, your customers and your organization.

Here's another thought, and I'm not sure you'll subscribe to this, but I'll say it anyway. Do not just try to get feedback on your leadership style using 'generic' 360 surveys and tools. I mean, don't just depend on questionnaires that ask your team—does your manager delegate authority to his/ her team members.

Don't get me wrong here. These 360 surveys and tools are very useful. But to my mind, they fall short of some real, hard-hitting and important stuff like trust, integrity, honesty and respect.

So here is something you could try someday—create your own 360 survey using websites where you can create free surveys (there are a few good ones that let you do that). Ask some real questions like—do you trust me? Do I disrespect you by using inappropriate language in office? etc.

My point is this—we sometimes have surveys that check things such as 'employee engagement' in a very indirect way. Why not check the things that really matter, directly.

You, as a manager, have a responsibility to develop the kind of corporate citizens that your company wants. So get concerned and watchful about how you act and show up, and what you say. Remember—Indian Parents have Indian looking Children. You decide what you reproduce.

YOU MAY NOT BE A BORN VISIONARY, BUT YOU CAN CONNECT THE DOTS

> The most dangerous leadership myth is that leaders are born-that there is a genetic factor to leadership. This myth asserts that people simply either have certain charismatic qualities or not. That's nonsense; in fact, the opposite is true. Leaders are made rather than born.
>
> Warren G. Bennis

Have you ever got feedback from your manager that 'you need to have a vision' or 'you need to be more strategic'? I have, and so I want to request those of you who've got the same feedback, or those of you who really think you're not visionary or strategic, not to worry.

My predecessor in the HR Manager role I do right now was a lady called Jayantika. Jayantika was excellent at coming up with new ideas. This helped her come across as quite a strategic leader. And she was, indeed, one. This was probably my single biggest worry as I took over her role. I thought—will my colleagues, and my company, accept me in her shoes while I know my 'vision, strategy' bone is not as well developed as Jayantika's?

Fortunately, over a period of time, I've learnt a few things. Some basic, some pretty cool.

I'd like to offer that there are two parts to being visionary or strategic.

The first is—connect the dots. When you just simply look around at the 'dots', you'll probably be able to connect them. What are these 'dots'? Dots are data. Dots are things you see around you in the company, within your team and in the marketplace that you operate in. Dots are things you hear and feel. Dots can be anything. Anything can be data.

Here's something you can do—take a topic, something that's bothering you, or even otherwise. Now think of all the dots related to that topic and put them all on a piece of paper. Once you've done that, look for trends, patters, and hence—possible solutions.

Let me give you an example. My team and I were having our annual planning meeting, one where we plan for what we would do in the coming year. We asked ourselves the regular questions whenever we're doing such a meeting—what should be HR's contribution in support of the businesses we serve? Where are we headed? What did we do last year? What does the landscape look like in coming years? Etc.

As always, we had scheduled a day-long meeting. But there was a difference this time. Instead of asking the team to present strategies, plans, trackers and dashboards, we had the team think about and present 'dots'. We decided that if we had clarity about 'what's happening' (i.e. the dots), then we would be able to connect them, see a pattern, and the solutions to our challenges would somehow emerge. This, to my mind, is a simple way of being 'strategic' and creating not just any vision, but a meaningful one.

Let me give you a little bit of detail on what happened from this meeting. While talking about 'Leadership Development', we saw some dots. Some of these dots were—there was a Director-level position open and five or six senior folks had applied internally. All of these applicants were very capable individuals, but only one of them got the job (obviously). The one who did get the job had never been at this position or level before. There was neither any formal or structured training that had prepared this guy for this job, nor was there any to help him now as he took over this role. Then, the folks who did not get the job were also high-performing leaders who had felt relatively 'stuck' in their current roles. There aren't too many opportunities to grow from where they were, and on top of that they did not get this one. So they probably felt bad about not growing where they were, and they probably felt worse not getting this job.

In another part of the business we had a bunch of new managers join us from other companies, and were feeling completely lost in the 'systems' of our company.

We also had many leaders in different teams taking on significant challenges for the company, yet feeling thoroughly unprepared to face those challenges.

Those were the dots.

When you put all of these dots together you start feeling—a lot of leaders need a lot of help. If that 'help' or support does not come at the right time, and in the right way, the results could be pretty bad—lack of motivation, poor results, frustration, and maybe that some of these good leaders will choose to exit the company and go work in some other company.

What did we do with all these dots and this understanding? We realized that we need to put something together to help and support such critical 'transitions' that leaders go through in the organization.

During this time I attended a program on 'Coaching' organized by a person that I highly respect. In that session I got introduced to the idea of an 'Internal Coach' program. In short, what this program means is that you train your senior leaders, those who have credibility in the system, to become 'internal coaches'. Then, you deploy them for various assignments, like—coach that 'x' manager who just became a Director in the company, or coach the 'y' manager who applied for the same job but did not get it, yet is a person we must retain in the company. We started feeling like a 'Internal Coach' program could help us achieve the goal of creating a support system for leaders going through critical 'transitions' in the organization.

You see what just happened? By putting the dots together you put down all that's happening, has happened, or is likely to happen. Next, you logically connect them. Finally—you look for something you can do about them. Together, I guess all of this combined can be called being a bit visionary or strategic.

Earlier I had said that I believe vision or strategy has two parts, and the first part is 'connecting the dots'. In the example I gave above I've also revealed the second part—keep your eyes open, keep listening, and keep talking.

After connecting the dots it was important to find a workable solution. If I had not gone to that Coaching program, I would not have known about the 'Internal Coach' program, which eventually became the viable solution to our challenge.

For a long time, in fact for many years, I resisted going to attend seminars and training programs where many people from many different companies came together; there were a few speakers, group discussions etc. I was part of a company that was already considered one of the best employers in the country, so I thought it was meaningless to go listen to people who are working in companies that are not in the same league as mine. I was wrong. I was very wrong, and I'm glad I'm changing.

Ideas that can become useful solutions can come from a variety of places. They can come in conversations with the most important people— your customers. They can come in conversations with people who've come into your company from other companies. Of course, like I mentioned earlier, ideas can come from listening to people from other companies in seminars, various industry forums etc.

Bottom line—you don't have to be a 'continually-creating-visions-and-strategies' kind of person. I think most people are not. What you can do is keep your eyes open, keep listening and keep talking.

Finally, something Jack Welsh said in one of his books stuck with me. He said something like—strategy is choosing what you want to focus on, and then making sure it gets done.

It's all about getting it 'done'. It's not about—I'm thinking about it. Like the saying goes—the proof of the pudding is in the eating. Companies care about results from meaningful actions. Companies don't care about ideas. So, once you've decided what to do, get the right amount of management buy-in and then get going.

Think about the dots and document them, see the patters, look for a solution, and look in many different places. Finally, get going and show results. Who knows, someday someone may say to you—you're a visionary, or that you're quite a strategic person.

A CRICKET TEAM NEEDS ELEVEN PLAYERS, NOT JUST ONE

Two are better than one because they have a good return for their hard work. If either should fall, one can pick up the other. But how miserable are those who fall and don't have a companion to help them up!
Ecclesiastes 4: 9-10, Common English Bible

When I was a kid I used to play cricket in school, like pretty much all Indian kids do. I was not a very good player, but I could do a bit of everything. This 'I could do a bit of everything' was a problem, as you'll read in a minute. Anyway, I did some batting, some bowling, and even wicket-keeping. I never became the captain of any team I played in, but because I was an overweight kid I was considered one of the big guys, and the big guys somehow always made it to the team.

As I got older I noticed something about myself, and others, with respect to trusting your team. There used to be times when my team had batted first and posted a certain score on the board. Then the other team would try and win by beating that score in as many, or lesser, number of overs. I noticed that if the other team needed just a few more runs to win and only one over (6 balls) were left to be bowled, then I thought we could restrict the other team and win, if only I bowled the last over. I could sense from the facial expressions of the other bowlers that they felt the same too.

Isn't this funny? There is hardly any logic to this self confidence. But somehow I thought that only I could bowl that last over so perfectly, such that I would restrict the batsmen of the other team in such a way that they would be mesmerized and paralyzed by my bowling, and would not be able to score any runs, and would lose.

Obviously I am not giving a lesson on the game of cricket here. I am really talking about holding yourself back as a leader, even when you think you're the best person to do the job, and trusting someone else to do it, even in that 'last over'. It can turn out that they (your employees) don't do the job as well as you do, but at least it'll mean they're on the way to eventually doing it as well as you do. I'm not saying all managers should always give up bowling that last over. No. Sometimes you do need to step in. Sometimes you do need to bowl that last over if your bowling will help your team and your organization win something really important.

I'm saying this—we, as managers, need to understand that perfection demands practice, and practice can happen only when sometimes we step aside, take a risk, and let our employees do the job (practice), let them make a mistake, and let them feel happy about doing what you allowed them to do.

This cricket example can be translated into anything else in a company—closing a deal, making a presentation, anything. The question is—do YOU have the guts to step aside and see your team develop? If you don't give them a chance to bowl that last over, they'll never learn what it is like to close a match.

I was once travelling to Malaysia, and in that week either I or a person in my team had to present one of our HR initiatives as an 'Innovation Entry' to a panel of judges whose job was to identify and reward the best innovation. The competition was undoubtedly tough, as innovators from other teams were also showcasing their innovation. At the end of this, whoever made a good presentation and showed great business results would win an award, and the associated recognition. The problem was that the panel of judges was a set of leaders who were physically present in the office in India, and presenters from various teams could choose to either present to them face to face, or present on the phone. The stakes were high and I was in Malaysia—not good. The option of allowing my team member, who could do this face to face in front of the panel, to present was like allowing someone to bowl that last over . . . . You know where this is going.

You don't have to bowl the last over all the time. Eventually, your aim should be to develop bowlers, while you can be on the field coaching and praising them. Your role is to give them the shot, take a risk, trust them, support them if they fail, give them balanced feedback, and applaud them for their effort.

If you try to be all the 11 players of your team all the time, you'll eventually exhaust yourself, and develop no one. The strength of your team will stay concentrated in you, and someday you will lose your 'business' to a 'competitor'. This is true even for a Human Resource team, like mine, whose customers are internal to the company.

COMMANDING RESPECT, AND REVERENT FEAR

For rulers hold no terror for those who do right, but for those who do wrong. Do you want to be free from fear of the one in authority? Then do what is right and you will be commended.

Romans 13: 3, New International Version Bible

The challenge of leadership is to be strong, but not rude; be kind, but not weak; be bold, but not bully; be thoughtful, but not lazy; be humble, but not timid; be proud, but not arrogant; have humor, but without folly.

Jim Rohn

Leadership is a strange dichotomy. You have to play many roles at different times, and some of these roles sometimes seem almost the opposite of each other. It's strange.

I once worked for a manager who I respected a lot. I fully trusted him. Yet, at the same time, I feared him. I think that was good leadership on my manager's part, and I explain this point below.

I think we all understand the concept of 'respect', but we don't fully appreciate 'fear'. I mean 'fear' from the perspective of not doing the job. How does your team feel when they've not done the job at the standard they should have and/ or by the time they should have? Do they feel they can 'get by'? Do they feel they can give you an excuse and you'll grudgingly buy it and move on without telling them that you don't appreciate it? If yes, then that's not good. They must have a respectful fear about not getting the results they should have.

This lesson also has the tendency to be misunderstood, so let me clarify. I don't mean to say people should fear coming to office, fear saying 'Good morning' to you, fear asking you if you'd like to go for a movie with them etc. Not at all. I think you should hang out with your team once in a while if you can.

But here's the point—I can hang out and see a movie with an employee of my team tonight, but if there is a deadline tomorrow, I must/ will ask him, point blank, if he has done the job or not. And if he has not, then hanging out with me and having a personal relationship with me will not come in the way of me holding him accountable for his lack of accountability. This should be clearly demonstrated by you, and understood by your team.

Way too many managers want to be 'good friends' with their team members, and that's ok. What's not ok is letting that come between your role as a manager, and the results you have to get achieved through them. Friendship is an enabler, it's not the objective. Being friends is good, and it helps, but it's not the goal of being a manager. You get paid to be a manager not to make friends, but to get things done.

How do you balance this? Well, you have to find your own way. What works for one manager may not go well with the style of another manager.

However, here are some ideas on how you can develop friendship and respect with your team—if they are hungry to achieve, then give them something meaningful to do. Sometimes coach them; sometimes just get out of the way. When they make a mistake, protect them. Take the blame on yourself if need be. Don't lie, but just don't let anyone know who actually made the mistake. Remember their birthdays, and do something special. Remember their anniversaries, and make sure you don't allow them to work that day. Remember the date they joined the company, and celebrate those anniversaries. Don't wait for a person to serve 5 years in the company to tell him/her that you're thankful to them for accepting your job offer.

Just do whatever you can. Whatever goes with your style, and suits the employee, works. Every person has a different need, I believe, so think of doing something special for them. Every person is in a different phase of life, so try and understand that and make things special around that.

How do you make sure they have a respectful fear of you? First and foremost, in your words and actions, make it clear that results matter the most to you. Have the courage to look them in the eye and say 'you were supposed to complete this. You've not. I don't appreciate it'. Of course, don't do this every day for everything. Even when you are saying these words, say so respectfully. You don't have to be angry and you don't have to raise your voice.

You have to remind your team that being successful is very important to you, as it should be for them. People want to win, so they will align with this message soon. Create a 'performance driven' culture in your team. Success is a great motivator. When, through your leadership actions you create a successful team, then you won't have to worry about people leaving you just because they had a bad day or just because you were tough with them one day.

Sometimes when you see behavior that you must discourage, a tough conversation with the employee is what is needed. Be direct, be tough, and yet be respectful. But again-be direct.

There was a time once where a few managers reporting into me were not collaborating enough and that was affecting the overall performance of the team. I remember saying to each of them separately 'if I don't see collaboration between you all, then it will impact your rewards and your ranking'. This is as direct as it can get. I told each one of them that they will not get a good rank at the end of the year, and they will not get great increments, if they continued to act in this non-collaborative fashion. I didn't mean to threaten my team, but I really meant what I said. When things get really serious (like it got in this case) then giving the message as clearly and directly helps.

Sometimes when I feel someone reporting into me 'dropped the ball' on something critical, I simply ask them 'because you did not spend enough time on this work, what do you think our customers will think about us (the team)'. That question is usually enough for them to get the message and start focusing.

On a similar note, I highly recommend that you should try never to cancel your regular review meetings with your team. When you do that often, people feel unaccountable towards their work.

Eventually they'll see you as a person who gives the work, but then does not care enough to follow up or review. Bottom line—they'll feel the goal was not important enough, and you don't care. This depletes respect and fear.

Finally, make sure your team knows the real definition of performance. It is—job done. Not 'job still doing'. Not 'trying our best'. Not 'project underway', but project 'done'.

I can go on and on about this topic, but I'll stop here and I hope you get the point.

I'm sure you love socializing with your team, and you should. In some way they are your family, and you probably feel very nice being with them. You should want to be their friend. They should feel comfortable sharing concerns with you. I'm sure you feel nice talking to them, knowing about what's happening in their life. But they should be clear that you don't like them not doing their job, and be clear that the two sides of this leadership coin can never become one.

The fear they feel telling you that the job could not get done, when if they had done their best could have got done, is good fear. It'll drive them to do their best, and it'll make you all a very successful team.

REVIEW **<u>AND</u>** ASSIST, DON'T REVIEW **<u>OR</u>** ASSIST

Leadership is solving problems. The day soldiers stop bringing you their problems is the day you have stopped leading them. They have either lost confidence that you can help or concluded you do not care. Either case is a failure of leadership.

Colin Powell

Our job as a manager can be broadly categorized into two things—'Assisting' our employees, and 'Reviewing' the work they do. We cannot do too much of one; there has to be balance most of the time.

There was once an individual, a colleague of ours, who I and my team used to work with quite a bit. He was at a fairly high position in the organization, and while he was not managing a part of my team (I was the direct manager of my team), there was one part of my team's job that he, in his role, was accountable to. Basically, while the team directly reported into me for all they did, there was one part of what they did for which this guy also needed to be informed and kept in the loop in, or needed to give approvals for. So, he was in a role of influence over one part of what my team did.

He and I had challenges working with each other.

The problem was that he always 'reviewed' the team, and hardly ever 'assisted' them. My team would tell me how he would ask too many questions in a tone that sounded as if he was 'suspecting' them. They told me how he never made an effort to really connect and understand their situation, but had all the energy to ask them why they had not been able to finish a certain task. I observed and watched him too, and saw that he did not even want to understand the challenges my team was facing, and how he would get all flustered if something had not got done.

I think 'reviewing' your team is an absolute must, because at the end of the day, the work needs to get done. You must ask the questions—has the work been done? What process are you following?

What stage of the project are you at? These are all important questions we need to ask our team to hold them accountable.

But we can't ask them all these questions all the time. You must get flustered/ concerned, in a way, when something does not get done, but you must also take the time to understand why it did not get done. You must have the patience to listen for genuine reasons for non-performance, have the empathy to acknowledge the challenges faced by the team, and finally—assist them in overcoming those challenges.

Just imagine having a boss with whom all your meetings are 'review' meetings. How does that feel? Its simple—it feels like the guy is out to find something wrong in what you are doing, and is out to nail you. This review-only behavior does not create long-term commitment and engagement. In fact it creates a very suffocating culture.

While we need to review our team members to ensure work progresses, we also need to recognize that our team needs us to 'coach' them, to 'assist' them. Make each conversation with them about review AND assisting. If an employee is failing at some task you've given her, don't you think that employee needs some amount of 'assisting', maybe more than 'reviewing'.

I believe those managers who have an unreasonable amount of need to review their people are very insecure. They don't have the guts to fail while their team is learning new skills. It's sad and de-motivating to work for such managers. More than anything, it's very discouraging to work for someone who seems to be 'coming after you' for everything.

Your job is to get the job done, right? Your job is to get the results your company wants you to get through your team, right? You really think that happens only through reviewing your team's work? No—it happens when you assist them to do their job, and then review what and how they've done. You can't do one of these, you have to do both.

So, don't be just a reviewer. Eventually you'll be known as a pain to work with. Leadership is a balancing act, and if you can't do that, and all you do is review, then you're being an enemy towards the goal of long-term engagement and results.

FRIENDSHIP IS OPTIONAL, TEAMWORK IN NOT

> So the eye can't say to the hand, "I don't
> need you," or in turn, the head can't say to
> the feet, "I don't need you."
> 1 Corinthians 12: 21, Common English Bible

How do you deal with a situation where teamwork amongst the people who report into you is an absolute must, but it's just not happening? I am sure you have many good ideas of what to do in these situations. I have two suggestions to offer.

First—don't go crazy trying to make teamwork 'happen' in a matter of a few days or weeks. I mean—give it time. I think it's important to recognize that people take time to gel together, and that relationships take time to build.

Once I had a situation where the group of employees (who were Managers themselves) reporting into me just were not 'clicking' with each other. They were all very good human beings (they still are) individually, but as a group it just did not feel like they were a good team.

I did all I could to make sure they were a good team—I gave them all the right messages, I coached them individually, I 'caught' bad behavior that went against teamwork and I gave instant feedback, and so on. The problem was—I was overdoing it. I had set a goal in my mind that they need to work almost like a group of great friends in a matter of three to four months.

It just did not happen. I grew increasingly frustrated and irritated. I started becoming very angry around this topic. However, no matter what I did, show love or show anger, they still did not work like a well-oiled machine.

Then after more months than three, I realized my own expectation was the problem. In many different ways my team kept telling me 'don't worry, it'll happen, just give it time', and I was not listening.

I hope you won't make the same mistake. Putting people of different talents and personalities in one team is a good thing, but allowing them to thrive and work like a well-oiled machine does take time. In fact, trying to accelerate that process sometimes can be very detrimental. I saw there were times when my team members would visibly feel pressured to collaborate in order to show me they were collaborating. This created stress and disengagement, and I was responsible for that.

So what can you do? Talk about teamwork, but don't make people work in a team when clearly working individually will produce the same quality result as working in a team. For the sake of collaboration don't compromise speed. Encourage your team members to talk to each other and sort out their differences, but don't always force them to do so. Treat them like adults, not children. When one of them comes to you with a concern with the other, listen to them, rather than dismissing them by saying 'you need to talk to the person you have a problem with'.

Teamwork and collaboration is important, but even families have trouble. Sometimes we give time and space to our family members, and let time heal our differences. My learning has been that it takes time in a team as well.

My second piece of advice is that we managers need to understand that while relationship building takes time (as I learnt the hard way), a bare minimum level of collaboration & team work that is needed to get the job done is an absolutely non-negotiable thing.

Here I'd like to repeat an episode with my team, but it's important to repeat it in order to drive home the point I'm trying to make. During this time when my team was trying to learn to work with each other, and I was trying to be the perfect boss (I was far from it, as I've explained), there came a time when the lack of collaboration amongst my team members started affecting our team's results negatively. Deadlines would get missed because two people did not take the time to work with each other and close an action. Sometimes large projects would not get launched at the time we said we would launch because people just avoided each other. It was starting to affect my team's performance, and I needed to address that.

Here's what I did, and I encourage you to use this skill when you absolutely must (not anytime, and not all the time). I had a conversation with each of my team members separately which simply sounded like this—If you do not collaborate and make sure 'x' thing gets done, then it will impact your yearly ranking and rewards.

I know—that sounds like a threat. But I encourage you to think about this—you would anyway impact (negatively) someone's ranking and rewards (increment, bonus etc.) if they do not collaborate, and if that is causing your team's results to go down. If that's anyway going to happen, then why would you not give them a warning about it? I think it's fair you do so, and it gives a real opportunity to people to correct their behavior and align it to your expectations.

I think this is what it did in my case—I think my team got a direct view of the impact of their poor behavior, and got a direct view of my perspective of the consequences of such behavior.

Did it help? Yes, it did. With this one conversation I saw my team moving from 'conscious non-collaboration' to 'conscious collaboration'. I know 'conscious' collaboration is not the best place to be, but it's better than where we were before this conversation. I think when shown the mirror, people change. I heard somewhere that 'people change either when they see the light or feel the heat'. Said differently—people change either when they see an opportunity or when they're forced to.

If they're not changing when they see the light, then you must make them feel the heat. Collaboration and teamwork is just too important for you to not be honest and direct with your team about.

IT ONLY TAKES ONE FOOT TO TRAMPLE AN ARMY OF ANTS

"Don't be afraid," the prophet answered. "Those who are with us are more than those who are with them."

2 Kings 6:16,
New International Version Bible

Have you ever inherited a team and then been asked to 'cut' it to less than half its size? I have, and in the process I learnt a few valuable lessons.

I once inherited a team that had sixteen employees in it, full time as well as contractors. In a few months we had only seven employees left. It's not in how we did it that I learnt something; it's in what happened after we did it.

I realized that when we had sixteen people in the team (which was more than I think was needed), in trying to create work for all sixteen, over a period of time we had taken over doing useless activities that nobody cared anything for. Ideally one should see how much work is required for the customer and then staff accordingly. In our case it was the other way round—we create more and more work in order to keep everyone busy. A lot of the work that we were doing was created by us, sometimes without our customers really 'needing' it or seeing any value in it. The proof of that was that when we became a team of seven, we stopped doing a lot of the work we used to do, and nobody missed it.

First of all, every leader, every manager, and every team must ask themselves these questions regularly—What do we do? Who cares about what we do? What should we really be doing? How can we add more value? What can we do to make our customers more successful?

When this transition, that I started explaining above, was going on, we realized that our true value as a Human Resource team was not in the low-end stuff we were doing. The low-end stuff included things like pulling data for line managers (something we could teach them how to do), answering queries asked by employees (something we could document and publish for their ready reference), conducting interviews for hiring entry-level employees etc.

We realized that our real value was in 'consulting' with the business managers. We realized that if we truly had to make a real difference, then we needed to engage with senior line managers and work with them on their toughest people challenges, things like compensation management, succession planning, senior level hiring, performance management, etc.

With that clarity, and I have to say—you must be clear, we realized two things—(a) we needed more senior/ experienced HR professionals in the team, and (b) we did not need sixteen people. Bottom line—we needed a smaller, more capable Human Resource team.

We worked on this strategy, and over a period of time our businesses seemed to value our services more than they had in the past. They started engaging us more, and seeking out our advice a lot more. We started having a real seat at their table. By the way, cutting the team from sixteen to seven was not my decision—it was asked of me to do so. But in hindsight, it was a blessing in disguise.

So here's one key lesson—if you overstaff your team (i.e. beyond the required capacity) then you will need to look for or create work to keep everyone busy. In the bargain, you will keep picking up non-value added work, or create non-value added work for yourself. Eventually, the value your team provides to its customers will erode.

Like I said, the starting point is to be clear about your strategy. You can't be a 'strategic' function by creating a large team of low-skilled employees. When you are clear about your strategy, then you can accordingly right-size your team, and hire the kind of talent that will make your strategy become real.

The story does not end here. As you can imagine, when we reduced the team size from sixteen to seven, the people went away, but the work stayed. I mean we still had a lot of work to do, and now it had to be done by less than half the number of people. How did we do it?

One thing we did was map out all the work we do on two parameters, (a) Repeatability-how often is this work required to be done, and (b) how many people can do it currently.

We mapped every little thing we did against these two parameters. Mapping all of the work we do was the easy task. The tough part was to figure out what to do with all the 'work' that was highly repeatable. Well, the main thing we did was this (and I'm sure you get this already)—when some work had to be done a lot (very high repeatability) and there were very few people who knew how to do it, then we made sure we trained other people in the team to do that task so that there were more 'hands on deck' when we needed them. A good example of this is recruitments—recruiting happens all the time, yet we only had 1-2 people who knew how to do it. We immediately got the whole team to learn how to recruit. Now these 'extra' people who got trained to recruit were certainly not as good as the tenured recruiters, but they were good enough and could lend a helping hand in times of stress, i.e. increased workload.

So, we became clear about how we would like to add value (strategy), we right-sized our team, we hired the kind of talent we needed to make our strategy 'real' and finally—we trained people on critical activities so that we could do 'more with less'.

Lastly, we started doing something that I think all managers and all teams ought to do continually—make a 'Stop Doing' list. Every team, over time, starts doing things which seem like they add value, but really don't. Sometimes certain activities added value in the past, but they don't add any value anymore. Sometimes certain things do add value, but the amount of value you get is not worth the massive effort that goes into getting it.

Managers and teams must spend time every once in a while to evaluate everything they do, and then discard those low-impact, low-value activities that the team must stop doing. My team and I create a Stop Doing list at least once every six months, if not more often. This list does not have to be long, but even if you take away one thing every three months from your team's workload, it's that much time they can dedicate to doing something that will truly add value to their customers. It could a report someone is making, a certain series of meetings that are being held, or anything else. Whatever it is, if it does not add (enough) value, stop doing it, and focus that much energy doing something else.

When you are clear about how you and your team would like to add value/ contribute to your company, when you hire the right kind of talented people who can make that vision a reality, when you right-size your team, when you train enough people on critical activities, and when you take away the non-value added work from their plate, then you may realize that it takes just one foot to trample an army of ants.

PROVIDE AIR-COVER, ESPECIALLY DURING PHASES OF DEVELOPMENT

A man who wants to lead the orchestra must turn his back on the crowd.

Max Lucado

Imagine a scenario when you're trying to learn something new at work. As you learn to do this new thing you're doing, you make a mistake, as expected of any new learner. As soon as you make that mistake, your customer gets upset. As soon as your customer gets upset, your manager comes to you and says—I can't believe you goofed up. I don't want you to do this anymore.

How would you feel?

This chapter is not to drive home the point of patience or pep-talk. This is about providing air-cover for your employees, especially when they are developing.

I once had an employee (say X) who had been in the company, and my team, for a few years. He was a senior member of my team, a manager himself. He had been in an operations role before I took him in my team in Human Resource. After a few years of working with me, a different senior person (say Y) of my team left the company. I thought it would be a great development and a good change for X to take over Y's role. So I did that; within a few days X was doing a new job, which was previously Y's.

This new job was different, and even though X was a senior member in my team and in the organization, he did face challenges. One day, X made a few mistakes while working on a project for which the 'customer' was a very senior lady in the organization. The mistakes X did made the senior lady very upset. I was sort of in the middle—I felt that X did not make the mistakes intentionally (he was new to this job, was still learning), and I also knew this senior lady had a genuine reason to be upset.

This senior lady sent me a message saying how frustrated she was, how unaccountable X had been etc. (note—these were not the exact words she used). I apologized, and promised to look into the matter quickly. Things would have been ok if they had stopped at that, but they did not. This senior lady continued to send me messages saying how upset she was, how careless & irresponsible (again, these were not the exact words she used) X had been etc. Now this senior person knew that X was new in his role. However, the messages continued coming one after the other, and I kept saying sorry for what had happened in different ways. Finally, it got to a point where I started feeling like I needed to stop this onslaught.

Why did I want to stop this onslaught? Neither because I thought X had not made a mistake, nor because I thought this senior lady had no right to be upset. I wanted to stop this because in my view, people take time to develop, and while they are developing we need to show patience.

After a few messages were exchanged I wrote back to this senior lady saying something like 'you know this person is new in his role. I think you need to be more patient. It's not like he does everything wrong. He made a mistake, and I and he have apologized for it. Now we need to move on'.

Here's the bottom line—when people in your team are developing, sometimes you need to let your stakeholders, customers, and even your own manager know that they're developing, that everyone will need to support this development by being patient, and that you (the manager) will ensure that nothing very serious and critical will go wrong.

Many managers have the patience while their team is developing, but only some have the guts to protect their team from impatient stakeholders and 'management'. In times like these, we need to remind everyone that the larger objective is 'development', and that everyone has a role to play in it.

Now please note—you can't use development and patience as an excuse for non-performance. It's not like you can let a very large deal slip because you put your newest sales guy behind it. That would be unacceptable. But when it is appropriate and the task at hand is not a super-important one, then use those as opportunities to develop your team while providing air-cover to them.

Patience and tolerance from your end towards people who are developing is critical for their development. In the same vein, it's also important that you, as the manager, set right the expectation of those stakeholders and customers who might be impacted by work the 'developing' employee is doing.

Without your air-cover sometimes your employees may find themselves surrounded by angry stakeholders who would like to chew them to pieces. You need to step in and protect; the long-term benefit is just too sweet for you not to.

REAL DEVELOPMENT, NOT LIP SERVICE

> Before you are a leader, success is all about growing yourself. When you become a leader, success is all about growing others.
>
> Jack Welch

I once had a colleague who applied for an internal job at the company we were working for. If he had got this job, he would get a pretty good promotion along with it. He was a good candidate for the role, but someone better than him got the job. Understandably, not getting this job was painful for this person. To make it more painful, his manager asked him to work on some 'new projects' so that he would get more exposure and be 'more ready' the next time such a job came out.

In this case, these 'new projects' would make him an even better project manager than he already was. In fact, it was pretty obvious that his project management skills were already quite good for him to be even considered for this position. My colleague's manager was doing what I call 'lip-service-development'.

In cases like this you have to ask at least a couple of questions. One, how come these 'new projects' simply came about just when this person did not get the job? Where were they earlier? And second—what would these new projects teach the person that would make him really 'more ready' for similar roles later?

I think a lot of managers don't really understand what real development is. Real development happens on the job, and it happens while doing real work, real projects that are important for the company and for the boss. Usually 'invented specially for you' kind of projects are projects no one eventually cares about. They start off with some fanfare, and then are treated like a waste of time (because they are)

I've seen managers send their employees to 'Communication skills' training in the garb of 'development'. I'm not saying communication skills training are not good. In fact, some people really need it. But to use classroom training or meaningless projects as a replacement for real development does not help at all. In fact, it wastes everyone's time . . . . everyone's.

Here's a way to think of development—when you see the resume or bio-data of a person, it's usually full of 'real' work they have done on the job. It's full of meaningful projects they did for their company. It was real work, work that engaged and challenged them. It was like an acid test—they went through the experience and learnt a lot. That's the kind of stuff you see on a resume.

If that's the kind of work people get engaged with, get challenged from, and learn from, then that's the kind of work we need to give them as development. No fool puts 'attended communication skills training' in their resume these days.

I obviously don't mean that you give your new employees your company's most critical projects to run. All I am saying is that you should find a way to include your employees in stuff they'll get challenged with and work that's important for your function/ department's priorities. We need to trust our employees, that given certain boundary conditions, expectations, tools and resources, they do their best, and along the way—they learn.

There is another benefit to this approach of development. Sometimes we managers think of development as a monthly or quarterly activity, but it's not. Real development does not happen in a month or a quarter. It can take half a year, or a full year or many years to develop certain skills. By keeping your scope for development limited to small meaningless stuff, you will be challenged to think of something new to develop your employee on all the time. You'll keep thinking 'what can I give this person this month so that she feels developed?' This is inevitably going to be challenging for you. Rather, assign your employee to one or two key, meaningful, long-term projects, and then just manage his/ her development through those. Most of the stuff people put on their resume is stuff they did over a fairly long period of time, not stuff done in a month.

Development takes time. Sorry—'real' development takes time. Handing your employee something new to do every month and calling it development is not development, it's a waste of time, it's just 'more activity'.

In my career so far I have spent some money in attending various training and getting 'certified' as a facilitator on some of those. However, the 'certification' by itself did not make me a better person or a more effective leader. What has made me a more effective leader, I think, is the experience of having lived through numerous situations, like supporting my company during a recession. That's a very valuable experience. I gained an experience that a lot of people would never have in their life.

A real, meaningful development experience does three things—one, it teaches an employee lots of new things. It's real development. Two—it's good for the company. Eventually more people will know how to do critical tasks because more people were developed for it. Three—people become more 'marketable'. For almost 'nothing' (i.e. no cost to company), people can get developed when you choose the right development opportunity/ project for them.

And don't worry—not all people are waiting to leave the company once they feel they are 'developed'. Don't worry about involving your employees in meaningful projects because of the fear that they will leave once the project is over. Don't be so insecure. If they see you actively working towards their development, they'll value it. In fact, they'll worry about not having this kind of an environment in any other company. They won't leave if you develop them, they'll stay.

You should ask people who stay on in the same company for many years. They'll always say—I get the opportunity to learn all the time.

ARCHERY IS NOT DRAWING A BULLS-EYE AFTER YOU SHOOT THE ARROW

> Write down this vision. Write it clearly on tablets, so that anyone who reads it may run.
>
> Habakkuk 2: 2, The Voice Bible

I was once conducting a training program for a group of managers, and I think the topic was either 'Performance Management' or 'Coaching'. Part of the session was a module on 'Goal Setting'. One manager, a participant, raised his hand and asked a question. He asked—how do I deal with this situation—I have an employee in my team who thinks he is an excellent performer, whereas I think he is a below-average performer.

Think about it. In this case the employee thinks he/ she is performing at an X+1 level, while the manager thinks he is at an X-1 level. What's the problem? This problem is quite common, and it is that 'X' is not defined clearly by the manager. 'X' here stands for the goal or task, the expected result, the metric and its target.

If X is not clear, then everyone is left free to interpret whatever they want X to be.

Have you, as a manager, defined 'X'? Have you clearly defined the 'goal' for the work your employees are doing? I don't mean the vision; I mean a goal for everything you are going to hold them accountable for?

I once had a manager whose name is Chris Goh. Chris is an excellent leadership development professional. Chris once said—in archery, do you have a target to which you shoot your arrow? OR do you fire the arrow first, see where it hits, then go running there and draw a bulls-eye around it? Obviously, the first.

Giving specific, measurable, time-bound goals to your employees is not a good-to-do thing, it's a must-must-do thing. Why? It's because clear goals set clear performance standards. If performance standards are vague, then the 'X+1/ X-1' thing happens. Goals give people a purpose, a reason for action, and a reason to do their best.

If there's lack of clarity, nothing gets done because it's not motivating to work for something for which you don't know what the result and reward is going to be. People want to succeed and do well. In fact, a lot of us want to do better than our colleagues. All this can only happen when 'success' itself is defined clearly. Else, everyone will think they're at the X+1 level while you struggle to tell them why they're not.

Think of a football match without goal posts. Is that a game worth playing? No—it's a waste of time.

In summary—don't waste your time. Make sure you set clear, measurable goals for your employees. Then sit back and watch. Good players want to score that goal, and it all begins with having the ball under your feet and your sight on the goal post.

THERE IS NO 'YELLOW' IN ACCOUNTABILITY

Effective leadership is not about making speeches or being liked; leadership is defined by results not attributes.

Peter Drucker

The net-net message of this chapter is—Accountability is getting the job 'done'. The most important word in that sentence is 'done'. Notice that it's in the past tense. It's 'done', not—in progress, almost there, just about to get finished.

There are a few things about accountability and getting the job done that I think we need to be clear about. In your role as a manager, you 'manage' something. Most managers say—I manage my team. I think that's a wrong way of looking at your role. Your role as a manager is to manage the goals and expectations set by your company and its customers. You are not paid to manage your team; you are paid to manage the goals of your customers. Managing your team is a way, a part of the process, of managing the end customer's expectations.

If you get that concept, then let me ask you a question—does your customer care about a job that's 'done', or one that's 'almost done'? In fact, when you pay someone to get some job completed, do you care if they 'almost' do it?

What if you really needed to read the day's newspaper, but it doesn't come. You keep checking every 5 minutes or so whether it has come or not, but it doesn't. You call up the newspaper guy and he says 'I came to the place you live, but I realized I ran out of the newspaper you subscribe to'. How would you feel? Does that sound fair? No. Why? Because you paid for the newspaper to come at a certain time each day, and you just don't care if the newspaper guy came to the place you live or not. The result was—you did not get your newspaper.

It's just like that at work too. You and the team you manage have to deliver a product or service at the time and standard your customer has paid you to. As the manager of the team it is your accountability to make sure the job gets 'done'.

Which customer cares more about 'efforts made' than 'results achieved?' None.

I'm sure you've seen the traffic lights system of reporting that some teams and companies use. In this system, a 'green' light means 'job done', and a 'red' light means 'job not done'. So far this makes sense. What has never made sense to me is the use of a 'yellow' light. The fact that the yellow light is an excuse for not being 'green' is evident from the fact that on many reporting dashboards you see a few greens, one or two reds, and a bunch of yellows.

You know what happens here—you've not done something that needed to get done, so you're definitely not green. But you also don't want to mark yourself red, because that won't look good. That's where the yellow comes, and becomes a symbol of a job that's 'almost done' or 'still in progress'.

Once again—does a customer care about 'almost done' or 'still in progress'? Does your customer pay you for your yellows?

If you're a team that reports like this, then to start I strongly recommend that you take off the yellow color from your reporting formats and dashboards. In order to drive a culture of accountability your team must know that only two colors exist—green for 'done' and red for everything else.

You'll see that a 'green & red only' reporting also encourages a bit of healthy competition in your team. Everybody wants to have a lot of green against their name, and that's always a good thing.

As a manager, reward 'closure' more than anything esle. Reward a job well 'done', not a project 'kicked off'. In all this, track and report through greens and reds. If you become OK about having yellows, then they will become ok too. Soon, a culture of yellow will follow.

Finally, and this is the most basic thing about accountability', make sure you make it clear to your team that 'who' will do 'what' by 'when'. This is where it all starts. You can get exceptional results if there is clarity about who (which member of the team) will do what (the result that is expected of them) by when (the timeline by when these results are expected). Make sure this is clearly documented and communicated.

The way I've done this is by creating a file that has the columns 'who', 'what' and 'when'. This file is the main document that my team and I refer to in order to stay on track. Each month when we have our team meeting we spend a lot of time reviewing this file—who was supposed to do what by when, and has that who done it? The folks whose names are in the 'who' column give an update of their work, and we discuss outcomes. Based on the update we receive, we mark each activity a green or a red. Nobody wants to be red in that meeting, as you can imagine. By the way, a person can be green for a task in a month even if the goal can only be truly achieved say in 6 months, but he/ she has done enough in a month in order to be green in 6 months. So some of the green and red marking can be subjective, and that's where your decision-making as a leader will come in.

True accountability is not just about having a passion, it's about putting the passion into action, and getting the job 'done'. It starts with you, the manager. Make it clear to yourself and to the team that a job not done is a job not done. Don't hide behind a yellow.

THE JOURNEY TO BECOME LIKE YOUR ROLE-MODEL-MANAGER STARTS WITH BEATING YOURSELF

Everyone who's ever taken a shower has an idea. It's the person who gets out of the shower, dries off and does something about it who makes a difference.

Nolan Bushnell

When I do Management Development training for new managers, I often hear these folks almost hero-worship leaders they've worked for. Sometimes you'd hear a manager even say—I want to be as great a manager as X or Y (managers they have worked for/ are working for).

These are nice thoughts. In fact, at a certain level, these thoughts and comments display the humility of these new managers.

The part that makes me sad is that some of these new managers are burdened by the goal of being as good, or better, than someone they have seen or have worked for in the past. Sometimes 'that great manager' becomes the gold standard of leadership for these new managers, and they feel that if they can't be that good, then they'll never be good enough.

I narrate the following story to various groups of new managers about how my mentor, Mr. Srinivas (called Ch) helped his son understand that you really can't influence being better than someone else. Rather, the only thing you can control is getting better than yourself.

Ch's son was scoring in the 70s (let's make that up) in Mathematics. He came home one day and said 'I want to beat this girl in class in Mathematics'. Ch asked him 'how much did she score?' to which his son said 'in the 90s'. There was quite a gap, as you can see. Ch said to his son 'to get to the 90s, you need to get more than you got just now, then reach to the 80s, then 90s, and so on'. Ch asked his son to commit to study harder than before, in order to get more marks than he got this time.

The next time his son had a test, he scored still in the 70s, but higher than what he had scored last time. At this point Ch asked his son a very crucial question 'did you beat that girl this time, or did you beat yourself?' His son said 'I beat myself'. Then Ch asked him to study a little harder the next time so he could beat himself again. This is exactly what happened. His son moved into the 80s.

I don't know if Ch's son eventually beat that girl's 90+ score or not, but he certainly beat himself repeatedly, and moved from being in the 70s. The needle moved quite a bit.

The concept can be applied to leadership too. You can get better than yourself. You can take feedback, or simply reflect on your actions enough to conclude what in your leadership you need to continue, stop or start. You may or may not become as good a leader as that person you hero-worship, but you certainly can become as good as YOU can become.

I used to have a person in my team who was handling a very critical part of my team's operations—the management of the Provident Fund (PF) Retiral benefit of all employees. She had multiple responsibilities in my team, and PF Management was one of them. In this role, she had done a stellar job of transitioning the PF Fund Management from one vendor to another, and she had received a lot of appreciation for it. In fact, her work had got her and the entire team a lot of credit. I was very proud of her.

There was one problem though. She had a lot to do, and I thought she was struggling in other areas of her work that she was handling, not because she wasn't good at her work, but because there was too much to do. How I dealt with this situation has been a learning for me, and one which I'll never forget.

I basically decided I'm going to take PF Management away from her and give it to someone else in my team. One day I took this employee for a walk around our office campus, introduced this idea of giving PF to someone else, and quickly got her to say a half-yes reluctantly. The next day I announced this change to everyone—my whole team and some senior leaders in the company.

I had moved very fast. I was proud of myself. But I did not realize that I had moved too fast. Eventually not only did the decision prove to be a wrong one, but how I executed it was a disaster.

From my perspective I was helping her by giving her more space and time to do everything she was doing flawlessly. From her perspective she felt like she was being punished for doing something wrong which I was hiding from her. I thought I had her commitment when she said 'yes'. She, on the other hand, was only doing her best to comply with her manager's strong opinion.

I had made a mistake; a very big mistake. The 'hurt' I created took a long time to heal, and I was to blame for that. No matter what I said to cover-up my haste and immaturity, it did not help. No matter how many times I said to everyone 'she did a great job', I'm sure even they thought—then why did you take it all away from her in one day?

This experience taught me a few things; lessons I am conscious of now. The only silver lining in all this is that I've probably become a slightly better manager than myself, because I've not made such a mistake since then. I wish I had learnt this lesson from someone else's mistake, but that's ok.

All managers make mistakes. A good way to start becoming better is to look at the mistakes you've made and try not to make them again. That way at least you'll get better than yourself. Maybe someday, many years later, some new manager will say that he/ she wants to be like you. Maybe someday you'll score in the 90s. It doesn't matter where you are, the competition is you.

DON'T SACRIFICE CELEBRATIONS

Do not withhold good from those to whom
it is due, when it is in your power to act.

Proverbs 3:27,
New International Version Bible

I strongly encourage you to celebrate victories.

I know you're thinking—big deal. We've heard that before, and we do it often.

Well then, here's something more—don't forget to celebrate victories even when right at the moment a victory comes after a long tiresome effort, just then something goes wrong. Don't let the 'wrong' make you forget the 'right'.

I learnt this a few years back. I had started managing the staffing/ recruitment function of my company at that time. This was an add-on responsibility over my current job as the Learning & Development Manager. Now in my role as the Staffing Manager I was accountable to various metrics and targets. In particular, there were two metrics that had never been met together in a single quarter by the staffing team in the past, ever. These were called the 'Hiring Manager Satisfaction' score and the 'New Joiner Satisfaction' score. These were scores the hiring managers and new joiners gave to the staffing team through an online survey once a position got closed (candidate hired).

Like I mentioned, these two targets had never been met together in a single quarter, ever (or at least since I could remember). In fact, even one of them had hardly been met ever.

I and my staffing team decided to really go after these targets, and wanted to do our best at meeting/ beating them. We wanted to meet these targets, and meet them quarter after quarter. After being in the role for one quarter, we finally met one of these targets (the new joiner satisfaction score). We were determined to celebrate only when we got them both. So we waited for another quarter. We worked hard, we engaged with our customers (hiring managers), we gave them high-quality resumes, we reduced the time they had to spend interviewing by pre-screening all resumes well, and did some other things. We also engaged with our new joiners, the folks who accepted our offer of employment. We helped them understand their offer better, and we ensured they got a smooth hiring process.

Finally we felt confident that we'd meet these targets. I knew that if we met both targets in the same quarter just once, we would do it again and again. Success breeds success.

We were just a few days away from the day when we'd know how we did in the previous quarter. We were tense.

Just around that time, something really bad happened. Sharing of IDs and passwords is not something any company encourages. Each employee has his/ her unique ID and password for various systems and software, and each employee is expected to keep these confidential. However, what I did not know till then was that in my team people were sharing IDs and passwords to the system/ software we were using as part of the hiring and recruitment process. This was a practice prevalent in my team since even before I took over. On this particular day it turned out that a contractual employee in our team, by mistake, cancelled the requisitions of hiring managers across the world. This was bad; this was really bad. For one—IDs and passwords were being shared in my team. Second— requisitions opened by managers outside India were being cancelled by someone in India, for no rhyme or reason, using someone else ID and password.

It was so bad that there were many complaints. The week after this was found was very stressful for me, as you can imagine. A lot of people jumped in to point fingers, mandate corrective action and so on.

During these stressful days we got the data we had been waiting for, for months. We got to know that we met the Hiring Manager Satisfaction score and New Joiner Satisfaction score, for the first time in the same quarter. This had never happened before, and it was a big accomplishment.

But we did not celebrate. We were so bogged down by the goof-up that had happened that we chose not to celebrate.

What hurt me the most was that no-one higher-up even acknowledged such a wonderful accomplishment. They probably thought they'd be viewed as crazy if they congratulated a team for one thing, while the same team goofed-up on another.

My intent is not to criticize my higher-ups; they had reasons for what they did. But I decided that day to never let one loss influence another victory. If you fracture your leg the day your little child learns to walk, you'd still smile and clap for her I'm sure.

I guess as leaders we need to decide, intentionally, to keep our pain (of a loss) aside for a while till we finish patting the backs of our team members who make impossible things possible.

Finally, if you think you'll look like a fool for saying 'good job done' to a team that has goofed-up in a different area on the same day, then I strongly encourage you to check your guts and integrity. It's not about you looking like a fool; it's about them knowing that you see their contribution.

ARE YOU A FIRE HOSE OF NEGATIVE FEEDBACK?

You don't lead by hitting people over the head—that's assault, not leadership.

Dwight D. Eisenhower

None of us have an unlimited capacity to receive negative feedback.

Some managers have the tendency to convert any normal conversation into a 'negative feedback' conversation. These are usually presented as 'development ideas' meant to 'help' the 'poor struggling employee', but really these are conversations that feed the need of the manager to give negative feedback. In fact, some managers have a tremendous need to give a tremendous amount of negative feedback.

Before we move on to the main point of this chapter, let's stop and think about this—employees, including you (a manager) do not have an unlimited capacity to take negative feedback. So don't make every conversation a 'feedback' conversation.

Now let's move on—I'm sure you've come across these two 'managerial mindsets'—(1) I 'must' have feedback to give to my employees, and (2) if it's something negative I have to say, I can present it as 'developmental', and so I will come across as a keenly-observing and insightfully-smart manager.

The truth is far from this. You don't 'have' to have negative feedback for all your employees at any given point in time. Sometimes it's ok, and even appropriate, to say 'all's well, I don't have any feedback for you'. In fact, think about this—isn't saying 'all's well, I don't have any feedback for you' itself giving feedback? By doing this, aren't you in a way saying 'buddy, you're doing fine, don't stress, and don't change anything'. How many times have you said this to any of your employees?

In my role as an HR Manager a lot of people ask me 'do you have any feedback that I can work on?' I think too many people ask this question too often from too many people. Anyway, I tell most of these people the same thing—No. I don't have any feedback for you. I think when I say this, people probably have two reactions. At first they probably feel something like—what? You don't have any feedback to give (disbelief)? You must have 'some' feedback for me? You're an HR manager; at least you should have some 'readymade' feedback for me.

But I also think they have a second reaction a few minutes later. I think it goes like this—hmmm . . . . nice . . . . that's good . . . . I'm glad he did not give me one more thing to work on. I'm glad he did not add to the list of 'improvement areas' others have given me.

Hey—don't get me wrong. You can give feedback. It's your role as a manager to do that. And yes—sometimes feedback needs to be negative. That's all fine. All I'm saying is that you don't have to 'have' negative feedback all the time and you definitely should not 'give' negative feedback all the time.

I once had a colleague who reported into one of these excessive-feedback-giver kind of managers. This colleague of mine was telling me about his annual appraisal conversation with his manager. This is how my colleague summarized his conversation with his manager—The way my manager spoke to me, I felt like he was going to give me the worst ranking possible. It turned out that he gave me the best ranking. But at the end of our conversation, even I did not feel I deserved to be ranked the best.

That's how he made me feel. It felt like I could do nothing right.

Why does this happen? It happens because some managers have a 'need' to not focus on the positives. Some managers have a personal 'need' to come across as the smarter ones. They satisfy their need by being overly critical of their employee. In the process, they show the employee down.

Do you have these 'needs' too? Would you ever like to get so much negative feedback that it feels like you're drinking from the fire hose?

WANT TO BE SANTA CLAUS ALL THE TIME?

It is better to lead from behind and to put others in front, especially when you celebrate victory when nice things occur. You take the front line when there is danger. Then people will appreciate your leadership.

Nelson Mandela

One time, many years back, my manager got an offer to speak at a conference in Hong Kong. He asked me if I'd like to go in his place and be a speaker. I told my boss that a better person to go to Hong Kong would be a guy who reported into me at the time. I truly thought this employee of mine would be a better candidate for being a speaker at that conference than me, because he had done a lot of research on the topic of that conference. My boss agreed.

For about a month after that my boss communicated with the organizers of that conference. He always kept me in the loop on the progress, and always copied me on the eMails he sent to the organizers.

But the day everything was finalized and we knew that we could confirm to my employee that he was going to represent us as a speaker at this conference and that the organizers would pay for travel etc. my boss sent an eMail directly to my team member saying something like 'congratulations, you've been selected to speak at this conference, we're very happy' etc.

I felt so disgusted by the fact that he chose to send this eMail directly to my employee, rather than giving me the opportunity to give the good news.

In my frustration I started checking my eMails. I did that because I remembered that something similar had happened when I used to report to a different manager. I found the mails I was looking for. At that time too it was concerning this same employee of mine, just that my manager was a different person at the time. My manager at the time was considering getting my employee, this guy, certified to conduct a leadership program. Getting my employee certified to conduct this program would cost the company quite a lot of money, which included travel & lodging cost, certification cost etc. At that time my (previous) manager sent me a mail saying 'Zach, I would like you to communicate the good news to your employee'

A manager is responsible to giving his/ her employees all the bad and negative feedback, and all the bad and negative news. Then it makes sense that the manager also has the privilege of communicating all the positive stuff too. If you are a manager, and you have managers reporting into you, then please realize that those managers reporting into you have the challenge of communicating all the tough messages, so they should also have the opportunity to communicate the 'happy' messages like 'you've been selected for something' or 'you're being sent to represent the company somewhere'

I just think what my (new) manager did was poor management practice. If you are managing managers, and there's some good news for someone two levels below you, don't communicate. Let the direct manager of the employee communicate the good news.

You don't drop in when that manager has a tough conversation to do. Then why do you try to be Santa Claus at the wrong time and steal the thunder away from the direct manager? This is inconsistent leadership behavior.

What did I do in this particular scenario? I spoke to my manager and told her I did not appreciate what he did. I gave him my rationale of being upset.

Don't be inconsistent. If you expect your managers to handle tough situations, also let them communicate good news. At the end of the day you should feel happy that something good has happened; your goal is not to hog all the praise and recognition from all levels of employees under you.

YOU CAN'T PROMOTE WHEN YOU DON'T HAVE A POSITION, BUT DON'T LIE

"Just because something isn't a lie does not mean that it isn't deceptive. A liar knows that he is a liar, but one who speaks mere portions of truth in order to deceive is a craftsman of destruction."

Criss Jami

I keep hearing managers say—'everybody in my team wants to get promoted. I don't know what to do. If I don't promote them, then they'll leave. I have ten people reporting into me and all of them want to get promoted and become managers'

Every company has guidelines on how they promote people to the 'Manager' level. The basic criteria usually are past performance, leadership potential, a strong display of the company's values etc.

But I feel a lot of managers don't understand one thing clearly, and that is—you cannot promote someone if there is no role/ position into which you can promote them to. You cannot have two managers for a small team of say eight or ten people, and if you are already the manager of this team, then no one can be promoted unless you go somewhere. Period.

This is not meant to say—go somewhere so that someone else can take your job. This is meant to say—it's not your (nor anybody's) fault that there is already a manager for your team, and that's you. It's not your fault that a small team cannot have more than one manager. Hence, it's not your fault that you cannot promote anyone to become another manager in your team.

I sometimes do leadership development training, and once in a while I get a manager in the room who says 'what do I do? I have these people in my team who want to get promoted.' I ask the question 'can you promote them?', and this person says 'No, I can't. There's no place for another manager'.

That's it. An employee can have all the potential required to be a manager, his/ her past performance may be flawless, he/ she may be a poster-child of the company's values, but if there's no position to promote to, then there's no position to promote to. What can you, as the manager, do? To be honest— very little. My plea to you is—get this into your head and feel comforted by that. It's not your or anybody's fault. It's just how it is.

What can you do as a manger in this situation? Just go to your employee and say 'hey, I'm sorry, there's no position right now'. I know this is easier said than done, and some employees may not get this logic of 'there's no position, so wait'. I'm sure you have an employee or two who'll say 'this company does not grow people', or show similar negative reactions.

But once again—you can't do much so don't stress much about it. They want a promotion, you're the manager, there is no second management position, you can't promote them. It's actually, in a sense, a simple logic.

I'm not trying to make a joke out of this though. I'm not saying you should, from then on, completely stop thinking about the growth, development, and promotion of your employees. I'm not saying you should not try to place your capable employees in higher positions in other teams of your organization. It's your job to think about your employees' growth and development continually.

All I'm trying to say is—let the simplicity of this concept of 'no position, no promotion' de-stress you. You cannot promote everybody.

Now here's a caution. I've seen managers who start doing weird things when they feel 'pressurized' by their team members to promote them. Even though the manager believes that the concerned employee deserves a promotion, they don't tell the employee the truth. Instead, they go around looking for negative things or performance issues with this employee so that they can go back and say—here's stuff you still need to work on, so instead of asking for a promotion, work on these.

Every employee has areas of improvement and things they need to work on. As a manager if you cannot promote them you still need to ask them to work on their development areas. But don't go around unnecessarily looking for stuff this person has not done well, so that you can keep postponing the tough conversation of trying to explain that there is no position available at the moment.

Instead of wasting your time and energy on gathering data to 'nail down' your capable/promotable employee, say something like this—'Listen, I know you've done well, and I believe you have a real good shot at a promotion. You do have development areas, as we all do, but I don't think they'll come in the way of your promotion. But I also need to tell you the truth. You know that there is no position available right now. I know you can do the job at the higher level, but you'll have to wait for that higher level to open up. I do hope you'll stay with the company, and in my team. You're a real asset and I will keep doing my best to continue to develop you and to look for opportunities for you'.

Isn't that a nice conversation to have? Isn't that the truth? I think people are mature, and they will highly appreciate the honesty.

In summary—do what you can do. Develop your hi-potential employees, tell them the truth, and hope that they don't leave. Don't stress about what you can't do.

IF YOUR VALUES CHANGE AS OFTEN AS YOUR MANAGER CHANGES . . . .

Leadership is a potent combination of strategy and character. But if you must be without one, be without the strategy
—Norman Schwarzkopf

It is absurd that a man should rule others, who cannot rule himself
—Latin Proverb

Too many managers manage their people the way their manager wants them to manage. These folks are not managers, they're mere puppets.

The test of values does not come when things are all ok. Values are tested when times are testing. When that happens then do you lead keeping the company values in mind, or do you lead keeping in mind what would make your boss happy?

I used to once work for a very competent and strong manager. We used to have monthly team meeting where my manager expected everyone to be present. These monthly team meetings were scheduled at least a month in advance so that everyone could plan to be there.

In a certain month my manager reset the date of the monthly meeting to a date that I had already committed to my customers for something quite important. The re-set had happened so close to the actual date, that it was tough for me to go to my customer and say—I'm sorry, I can't do what I said I would do because my boss reset the date for our monthly meeting.

This was 'no big deal' kind of an example. As you can imagine, I spoke to my boss and told him I could not make it to our team meeting as I had already committed to do something for an important customer. He agreed reluctantly, but agreed. It was uncomfortable for me too, but I was clear in my head about what I wanted to do. I wanted to honor the commitment I had made to a customer.

While this was a simple example, sometimes, unfortunately, we also come across certain complex examples of managers who change their principles and values based on what would make their boss happy.

I used to work with a guy (my peer, same level as I was) who did what his manager wanted him to do, who did not do what his manager did not want him to do, who said what his manager wanted him to say, and kept quiet when his manager wanted him to keep quite. He hired the people his manager wanted to hire, and fired the people his manager wanted to fire.

He was a puppet, and everyone could see it. In fact, even he acknowledged that he was a mere robot, and his manager had the remote control. I remember speaking to this guy once when his manager wanted him to fire a certain employee from his team. This guy, this peer of mine, did not really want to fire his employee. But he did, because that's what his manager wanted.

When you change your values and principles to act like your manager wants you to act, you could unknowingly deplete value from the organization. We all know there are managers who want puppets in their team, rather than smart people. We can't choose our manager, but we certainly can choose to act in a way where our values and principles are not compromised.

People want to follow leaders who will stand for the values of the company, and show personal integrity in all situations. When you put aside all values, and are driven by the motivation to make your boss happy, then you're creating a culture where everyone will feel that to 'survive' they have to do what your boss wants them to do. It's sad, and it's very scary. When they see you act like a puppet, your team will think that even they need to act like puppets in order to survive in the company.

I hope you're not a puppet. I hope you'll stand up against things that go against the company's values, and your personal values and integrity. Don't keep your spine at home when coming to work. Open your mouth and speak up when you see something wrong happening. That's your job as a leader.

SOMETIMES GIVE YOURSELF THE BENEFIT OF DOUBT

I cannot give you the formula for success,
but I can give you the formula for failure:
which is: Try to please everybody
—Herbert B. Swope

Lead me, follow me, or get out of my way
—General George Patton

It's tough to be a manager.

Sometimes it's tough enough to motivate yourself to get out of bed and come to office, and then to motivate everyone in the team to get out of their beds, come to office and give their best is even tougher. When you're a manager all the mistakes all your team members make become mistakes you've made, because the buck stops at you. When someone calls in and says they're not going to able to come to office because their child is sick, you are the one who feels the pain. Sometimes it's tough to tell your employees that they have a bright career in the company, when you aren't sure about your own career in the company.

Give yourself a break. Put things in perspective.

Once, many years ago, I was having some trouble with one of my team members. To my mind, this person was being quite unrealistic in his demands. He wanted the company & me to sponsor a course for him that was quite expensive. I was not supportive at all, especially because I did not believe it would benefit the company in any way. However, after many conversations with this person on this topic, I started feeling a bit guilty, and quite stressed. Somehow I started thinking—am I doing the right thing? Am I being a good manager?

I spoke to my manager at the time and I remember how clear he was in his coaching to me. He said three things, and the first was 'If u start getting stressed about this one person on this one issue, can you imagine what will happen when you have a large team and each of them will have their issues?'

I remember thinking to myself then 'Wow. That does make sense'. My manager was not telling me not to handle the issue, he was just telling me not to let this one issue overcome my whole life. He was right.

The second thing he said was 'Have confidence in who you are. Feel more secure in who you are'

Right again. I was insecure about whether I was doing the right thing or not, and quite frankly, I was worried about losing credibility.

Finally, the third thing he said was 'Are you confident that you've done your best? If yes, then it's not your problem anymore. If your employee cannot accept your decision, then it's his problem'

It's true. If your employee cannot accept negative criticism, even though your intent was to help them, even though you criticized them constructively, then it's their problem. If you've done your best to develop and grow them, but they want more and more, and are being unreasonable, it's their problem. If you've done your best to pay your employees fairly, and they still feel they're being short-changed, it's their problem.

Quite a lot of managers want to win a popularity contest with their team. They want their employees to love them and to hero-worship them. Unfortunately, this motivation leads a manager to want to do everything perfectly. Unfortunately, you can't be a perfect manager. Many times you have to choose between doing the right thing for the organization and doing something that will make your people happy, and you have to choose the right thing for the organization, even though your employees may be unhappy.

Many years back I had a 'mentoring' session with a new manager where he wanted some tips from me on how to manage his old 'peers'. He said something to me, and he thought I was going to say 'very good'. He said 'whenever I take a decision, I first make sure I run it by my entire team individually, and when all of them are comfortable with it, then I announce it'. I did not say 'very good'. In fact, I probably said something to the tune of 'are you crazy?'.

This chapter is not about decision-making styles and skills. It's about saying—don't doubt yourself all the time. Give yourself the benefit of doubt sometimes. If you don't, instead of you managing your team, your team will be managing you.

ALIGNMENT IS <u>THEIR</u> RESPONSIBILITY

The key to being a good manager is keeping the people who hate me away from those who are still undecided.

Casey Stengel

I have asked more people to go (fired them) in my career for lack of alignment to our team's goals, than for poor performance or poor capability.

Sometimes we think we have a case of an employee who is not performing well, but when you dig deep you realize they have the skills to do the job, they have done the job right in the past, but they just cannot align with the goals you have set for them or for the organization for the future. Hence, they stop performing at the level you expect them to.

I once had an employee who just could not agree to how I wanted to 'measure' how we were doing as a team. I believe that the way we measure ourselves determines the way we act, and the way we act determines how we are perceived by our customers. In this case that I've started explaining, we used to measure ourselves on metrics that really did not make sense to the businesses we were supporting. We could somehow look good (there are always ways to slice & dice the data the way you want, right?), but whenever we presented our data, people would laugh at us. Poor performance can be easily hidden, and over a period of time we had found many ways of hiding our non-performance.

I wanted to change that. I wanted to put the 'real picture' out in the open, so that we could come across as a team that told the truth, and one that was committed to make a change and improve our performance.

Anyway, this particular employee just would not agree/ align. He gave me a thousand reasons why we should not change. I spent hours and hours explaining why we needed to change. However, he would continue to track and present data and metrics that were meaningless, and quite frankly, useless. My decisions at that time obviously did not go well with him, but he was unwilling to let go of the past and embrace the new way. This attitude started showing up in his performance as well.

Eventually, I had to let him go. There was no way I was going to carry on with him if he did not accept and align to the new way in which I wanted to measure and report our team's performance.

One can say that 'alignment' is a manager's responsibility. It's partly true. A manager needs to communicate the change, show the benefits of the change, try and get people along etc. That's good. But at some point 'alignment' becomes the employee's responsibility. A highly skilled employee who is not aligned to the objectives of the organization or the team is like a brand new, well polished, shoe that does not fit. If it does not fit, it does not fit. Period. It has no place in your house.

The phrase 'you don't get to choose your boss' is really true. Why? Because it is true that if you get a new boss, YOU have to align to him/ her. You really have no choice. You have to do your best to get on her/ his bus, and ride along. New managers, and experienced managers in a new team/ situation, struggle with this quite a lot. But one needs to realize that the job of a manager is to provide the strategy and the direction. The job of the team is to execute. It's not the other way round. The manager does not have the responsibility of aligning herself to the team's vision and strategy; rather, the team has the responsibility of aligning itself to the manager's vision and strategy.

Now, hopefully, as a manager, you'll come up with the vision, strategy, or direction that's sound (makes business sense). That assumed, it's the team that needs to align themselves to it. Some managers worry too much about creating alignment and give way too much time for the team to get aligned. When given too much time, the team really does not get aligned. Instead, in that long period of time the position of the manager weakens further and customers don't get the service they should. Time is wasted.

If, as a manager, you have done all you could possibly do to seek feedback from the customers, create a vision and made a plan, communicated that, spent time explaining it, asking questions, giving answers etc., and still someone on your team is not aligned, you must give them the message that 'this is how we're moving forward, and you need to come along'. If you find this employee just not coming along, then he/ she needs to find some other bus to ride, because you don't have time to waste.

Alignment is key. Once again—most people do a good job when you give them the right goal, the right tools and resources, tell them what they can and cannot do etc. But what separates the early-starters with the dead-wood kind of people is alignment.

In my view, when customers are not aligned to your goals, then you talk to them, you listen to them, you tweek your goals and strategies. Bottom line—you spend time. When your own team member is not aligned to your goals and strategies—don't waste your time trying to fit the shoe that's not your size. Your customers will tell you 'you don't have that much time'

ARE YOU STILL ADDING VALUE?

People who enjoy meetings should not be in charge of anything.

Thomas Sowell

Are you still adding value? This is a tough question to ask, especially to yourself.

I've been in roles where sometimes I've felt I've been around too long. I remember this one role I was doing where I had a fantastic, extremely competent, team. They were doing all the work that was required to be done, and they were doing it all well. I used to come to work, do one or two reviews and then just sit back and think about how else I could contribute.

Unfortunately, in my feeling of 'I am not contributing enough', I started to do some weird things. I don't mean unethical things, I just mean unnecessary things. For example, I would look at the work my direct reports were doing, and see what part of their work I could take on. Then I would go to them and say—Hey, would you like me to do this, and maybe you can focus on more important stuff?

Inevitably, they would say-sure. Who can say 'no' to the boss on a question like that?

Now I don't mean to say that sometimes taking some workload off your team and doing it yourself is a bad thing. In fact, when your team truly is stretched, the manager also needs to get her hands dirty. But taking work from them because you don't have much to do is a sign that maybe it's time for you to do something different, that maybe you need to free up your 'chair' for people under you to grow.

The other thing I started doing, and I've seen other managers in my situation do the same, is that I inserted myself as an 'approver' for various things. It's a simple logic right—I don't have much to do, so let me become an 'approver' for what others are doing. After all, I'm the boss and I have the authority to approve everything.

I'm sure you see the 'wrongness' in this. When you have to create work to keep yourself busy, you're probably at that stage in your role where you should really be doing something else.

A colleague of mine once said that when we (managers) start approving things that our teams can work on even without our approval, then we take away the agility from the system. Imagine if every manager becomes an approver for everything—nothing would ever move.

Usually we start off in a role with very high energy and enthusiasm. We contribute, we give ideas, and we get work done. But we're also learning ourselves, and learning takes time. In the role I described above, it took me about 3 years to get to a point where I could really say—I know my job. How did I know I knew my job? Well—I would come to office and could easily solve problems. I would get 100 eMails a day, and I knew the answers to the questions people were asking me in those eMails. How did I know I knew my job? I just knew it. I felt it. My job was easy and comfortable.

In fact, I started really enjoying my life. I started leaving office on time, spending more time with my family and spending time on my hobbies. It was a good time.

However, it did not last that long. I had all the time and space I needed, but I did not feel challenged. To be honest, I did not feel I was contributing enough. When I thought of how I can take my department and its contribution to the next level, I could not think of anything. I don't mean to say that anything was broken. Not at all. I mean, my team was doing well. The problem was—I personally was not doing anything to take my team to a different level.

Anyway, I could stretch this time (good life, but not very productive at work) for about a year and a half. Finally, at the 4.5 year mark (in that role) I decided it's time to move on to a different role in the company.

Sometimes it's good to move on. It's not because the role you're doing is bad, nor because you are incompetent. It's just that sometimes the role would be done better by someone else who has new ideas, new ways of doing things, new ways of looking at things. It's good for the role, the team, and the company.

I was once trying to tell a team member of mine that he needed to do things differently if he wanted my job. He turned around and said—I won't do your job the way you are doing it, so why should I change. That was an eye-opener for me. He was right. Everyone does their work differently, and it's in those differences that we find innovation and ideas. Sometimes it's good to recognize that you've done your best when it was your time, and that now it's time to hand the baton to someone who'll do the role differently, and maybe even better than you.

I'm not asking you to start looking for a new job every 3 or 4 years. I'm challenging you to ask yourself these questions—Am I the best person to do my role now? Does the company need a different person? Am I being fully utilized in this role now? Am I as good for the role now as I was when I first started?

And observe yourself—are you giving 'approvals' where none is really required? Are you creating work in the system for you to fill up your day? Are you calling meetings that are completely unnecessary so that you feel you've done something? Are you asking your team to re-do their work even though what they've done is good enough, but you'd like more and more reviews?

Do yourself a favor—either reinvent yourself to do your current role better, or let someone else do it, and you move on to do something where you'll once again feel like you're 'on top of your game'.